s ire to
th

The Greenwich Guide to
Time and the
Millennium

Graham Dolan, Royal Observatory, Greenwich

Heinemann
LIBRARY

GREENWICH
MERIDIAN
2|000

Any words appearing in the text in bold, **like this**, are explained in the Glossary.

First published in Great Britain by Heinemann Library
Halley Court, Jordan Hill, Oxford OX2 8EJ
a division of Reed Educational & Professional Publishing Ltd.
Heinemann is a registered trademark of Reed Educational & Professional Publishing Limited.

OXFORD MELBOURNE AUCKLAND
JOHANNESBURG BLANTYRE GABORONE
IBADAN PORTSMOUTH NH CHICAGO

Designed by Susan Clarke
Illustrations by Jeff Edwards
Printed in Hong Kong by Wing King Tong Co. Ltd.

03 02 01 00 99
10 9 8 7 6 5 4 3 2 1

ISBN 0 431 00697 0

British Library Cataloguing in Publication Data
Dolan, Graham
    The Greenwich Guide to Time and the Millennium
    1. Time – Juvenile literature 2. Calendar – Juvenile literature
    I. Title
    529
    ISBN 0431006970

Acknowledgements
The Publishers would like to thank the following for permission to reproduce photographs:
Bridgeman Art Library: pp41 (upper), 44, Giraudon p40; British Library: p15 (middle); Francisco Diego: p42; Robert Harding Picture Library: M Bolster p37; National Maritime Museum: pp4 (upper),10, 11 (lower), 14 (all), 15 (upper, lower),16 (both), 17 (both), 19, 20, 22 (both), 23 (lower), 24, 26, 28 (both), 29 (all), 31 (both), 36, 45 (upper right, lower); Powerhouse Museum, Sydney: p23 (upper); Science Museum/Science and Society Picture Library: p12 (both), G Bernard p34, NASA p5, D van Ravensway p4 (lower), F Sauze p11 (upper); Sipa Press: I Simon p45 (upper left); Studio Carr Ltd: p37 (upper); Syndics of Cambridge University Library and the Director of The Royal Observatories: p27; John Webb: p41 (lower).

Cover: Chris Honeywell (centre), National Maritime Museum (upper left, upper right), Detlev van Ravenswaay/Science Photo Library (lower left), NASA/Science Photo Library (lower right).
2 logos: © National Maritime Museum (1999)

Every effort has been made to contact copyright holders of any material reproduced in this book. Any omissions will be rectified in subsequent printings if notice is given to the Publisher.

Contents

The Earth –
our Timekeeper

Hundreds and thousands of years

A period of 100 years is called a **century**, whilst a period of 1000 years is called a **millennium**. Very few people who are alive today will live long enough to celebrate their 100th birthday, but most will still be alive in the year 2000, and will take part in celebrations welcoming in a new millennium.

The Millennium Dome at Greenwich, London, under construction in 1998.

The length of a year

Our year is based on the length of time it takes for the Earth to go around, or **orbit**, the Sun once. The further a planet is from the Sun, the longer it takes to complete one orbit. If the Earth was as close to the Sun as the planet Mercury, each of our years would be about a quarter as long. If on the other hand we were as far away as the furthest planet Pluto, each of our years would be about 250 times as long – and, if that were the case, you wouldn't live to see your first birthday!

Sun

Earth

Our solar system.

4

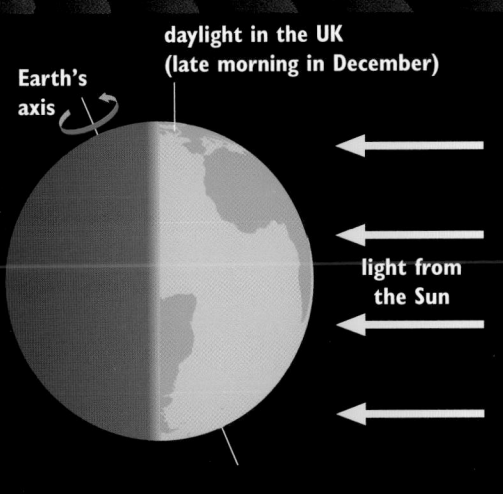

Earth's axis

daylight in the UK
(late morning in December)

light from the Sun

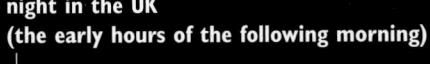

night in the UK
(the early hours of the following morning)

light from the Sun

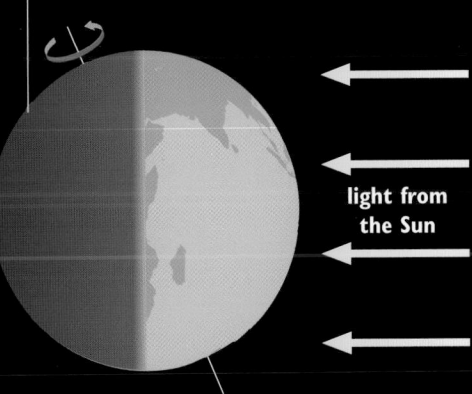

two-thirds of a turn later

Half the Earth is always in darkness.

The Earth spins round on its axis just over 365 times in the time that it takes to orbit the Sun once.

Day and night

At the same time as it orbits the Sun, the Earth is spinning on its **axis**. When the part of the Earth we are on is facing towards the Sun, we receive light and energy from the Sun, and call it daytime. As the Earth spins we eventually end up facing away from the Sun. When this happens, light and energy from the Sun can no longer reach us: it goes dark, and night begins.

The Earth photographed from space – the left hand side is facing away from the Sun and is in darkness.

The number of days in a year

The length of time that we call a day, is just about the same as the time it takes for the Earth to spin around once on its axis. Each day is divided into 24 hours, each hour into 60 minutes and each minute into 60 seconds. In the time that the Earth takes to orbit the Sun once, the Earth spins on its axis just over 365 times. To cope with the fact that the length of a year is really about 365¼ days, some calendar years are given 365 days, whilst others, called **leap years**, are given 366. These normally occur every four years. If the Earth was spinning faster, our days would be shorter and there would be more of them each year. If on the other hand it was spinning more slowly, our days would last longer, each hour, minute and second would be longer, and our clocks would have to tick more slowly.

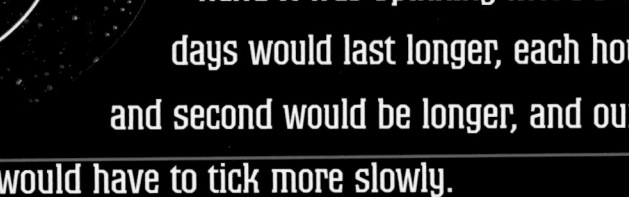

Sun

Summer and Winter

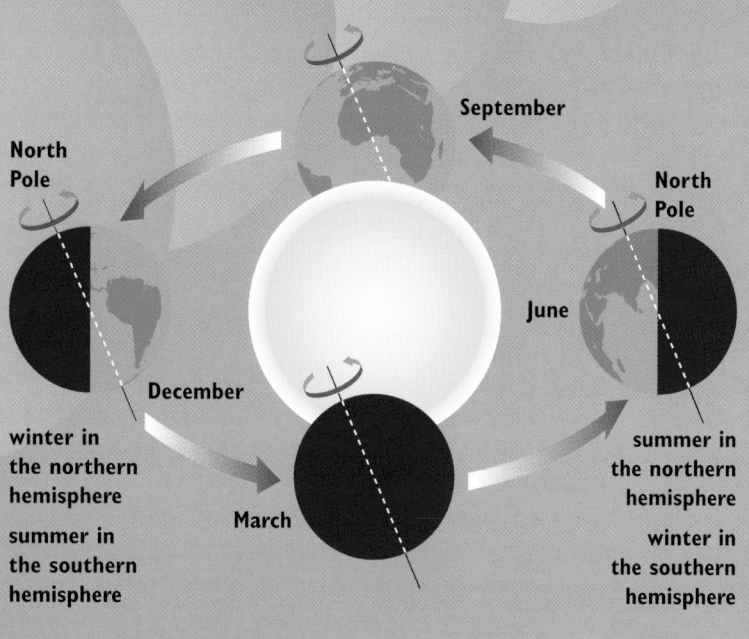

September

North Pole

December

winter in
the northern
hemisphere

summer in
the southern
hemisphere

March

June

North Pole

summer in
the northern
hemisphere

winter in
the southern
hemisphere

The Earth leans as it makes its journey around the Sun. As the Earth moves around its **orbit**, the direction in which its **axis** points scarcely changes. This means that when it is on one side of its orbit, the North Pole points towards the Sun, and that when it is on the opposite side of its orbit, the North Pole points away from the Sun and the South Pole points towards it.

Summer and winter are at different times of the year in the northern and southern hemispheres.

Hot and cold

When the North Pole points towards the Sun, people in Europe, Canada and other places in the more northerly parts of the northern hemisphere, called the northern **temperate zone**, get warmer weather. When it points away from the Sun, they get colder weather. We call the period of warmer weather summer, and the period of colder weather winter.

The more hours of daylight there are each day, the greater the amount of energy received from the Sun.

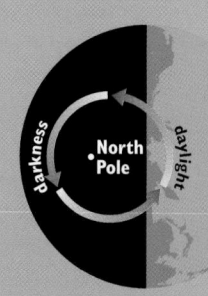

darkness

North Pole

daylight

When the North Pole points away from the Sun (December), people in the northern temperate zone get less hours of daylight than darkness each day.

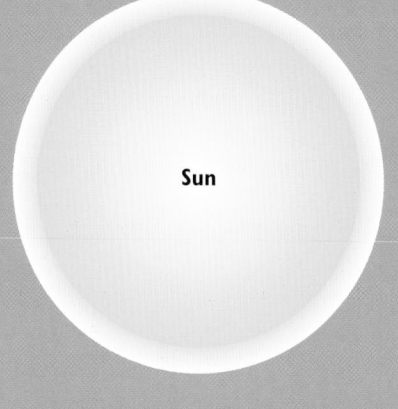

Sun

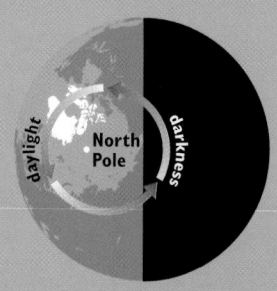

daylight

North Pole

darkness

When the North Pole points towards the Sun (June), people in the northern temperate zone get more hours of daylight than darkness each day.

Why though, should it be hotter or colder, just because the North Pole is pointing towards or away from the Sun? In the northern temperate zone, when the North Pole points towards the Sun, there are more hours of daylight each day, and the Sun rises higher in the sky. This means that more energy is received each day and it is hotter.

In countries in the southern temperate zone, such as Uruguay and New Zealand, summer occurs when the South Pole is pointing towards the Sun. When this happens, the North Pole will be pointing away from the Sun, and the countries in the northern temperate zone will be having their winter.

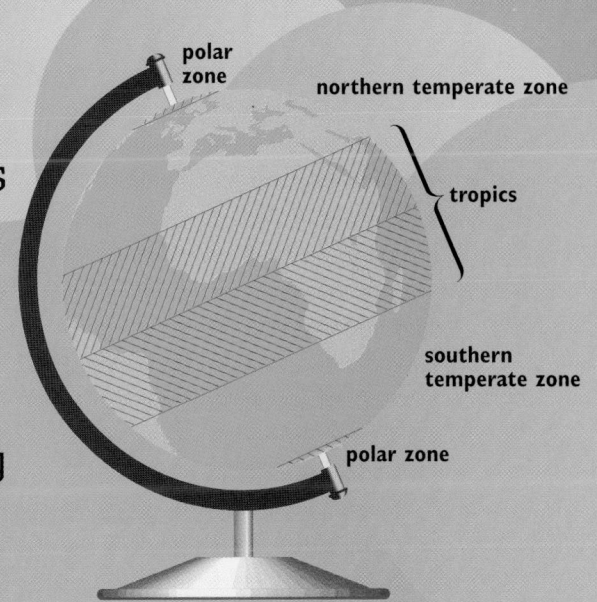

polar zone

northern temperate zone

tropics

southern temperate zone

polar zone

When the Sun is higher in the sky, its energy is concentrated over a smaller area of the Earth's surface – so it will be warmer.

The solstices and the equinoxes

In the northern temperate zone, the summer solstice occurs around 21 June, and the Sun reaches its highest **midday** point of the year. Six months later, on roughly 21 December, the winter solstice occurs and the Sun reaches its lowest midday point of the year. The amount of daylight increases each day between the date of the winter solstice and the date of the summer solstice. It then starts to decrease again. Roughly halfway between the solstices around 21 March and 22 September, the equinoxes occur and everyone across the world gets equal amounts of daylight and darkness. In the southern temperate zone, the Sun reaches its highest midday point in December and its lowest midday point in June.

The Sun's Movement
Across the Sky

The Sun appears to move from east to west

As the Earth spins on its **axis**, the Sun and the stars appear to move across the sky in a curve from east to west. At **midday** in the northern **temperate zone**, the Sun is in the south and the shadows point towards the north. In the southern temperate zone, things are the other way around. The midday Sun is in the north and the shadows point towards the south.

In the **tropics**, things are rather different. The midday Sun is in the south during the period around 21 December, but in the north during the period around 21 June. On the **equator**, the midday Sun is directly overhead at the time of the equinoxes in March and September.

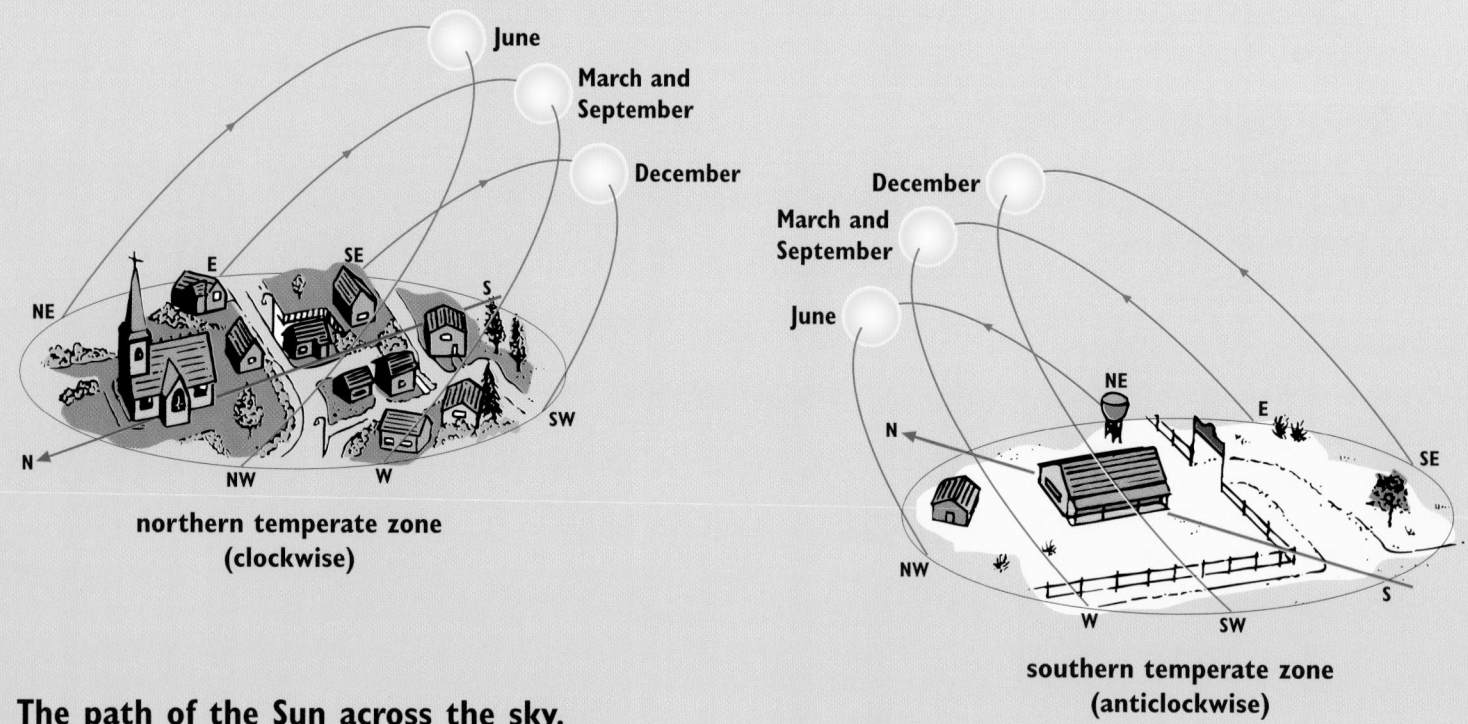

northern temperate zone
(clockwise)

southern temperate zone
(anticlockwise)

The path of the Sun across the sky.

Shadows

As the Sun rises in the sky, the length of a shadow gets shorter and shorter. By midday, when the Sun is at its highest point of the day, the shadows are at their shortest. They then start to get longer again, increasing in length all the time until the Sun sets. As the Sun moves across the sky, the direction of the shadows changes as well. The shadows are always on the opposite side to the Sun. In the morning when the Sun is in the east, the shadows point towards the west. In the evening when the Sun is in the west, the shadows point towards the east.

Meridian lines

No matter where you are, the shadows at midday always fall along a north–south line. One end of the shadow points towards the Earth's North Pole, and the other end points towards its South Pole. North–south lines are known as **meridians** or meridian lines. They are very important when finding the time from observations of the Sun or the stars.

The length and direction of a shadow depends on where the Sun is in the sky.

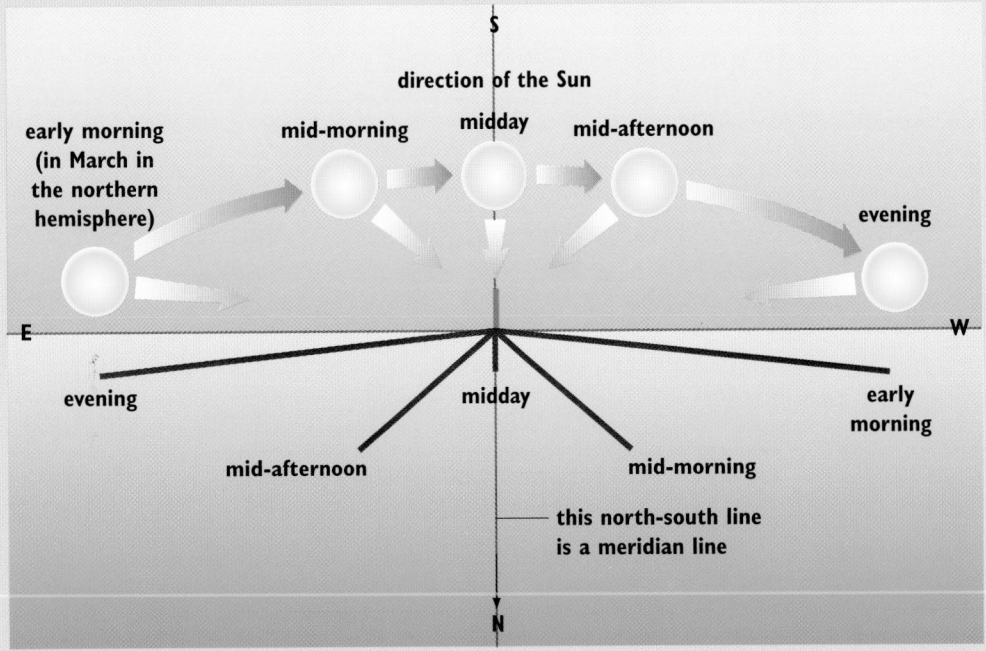

Sundials

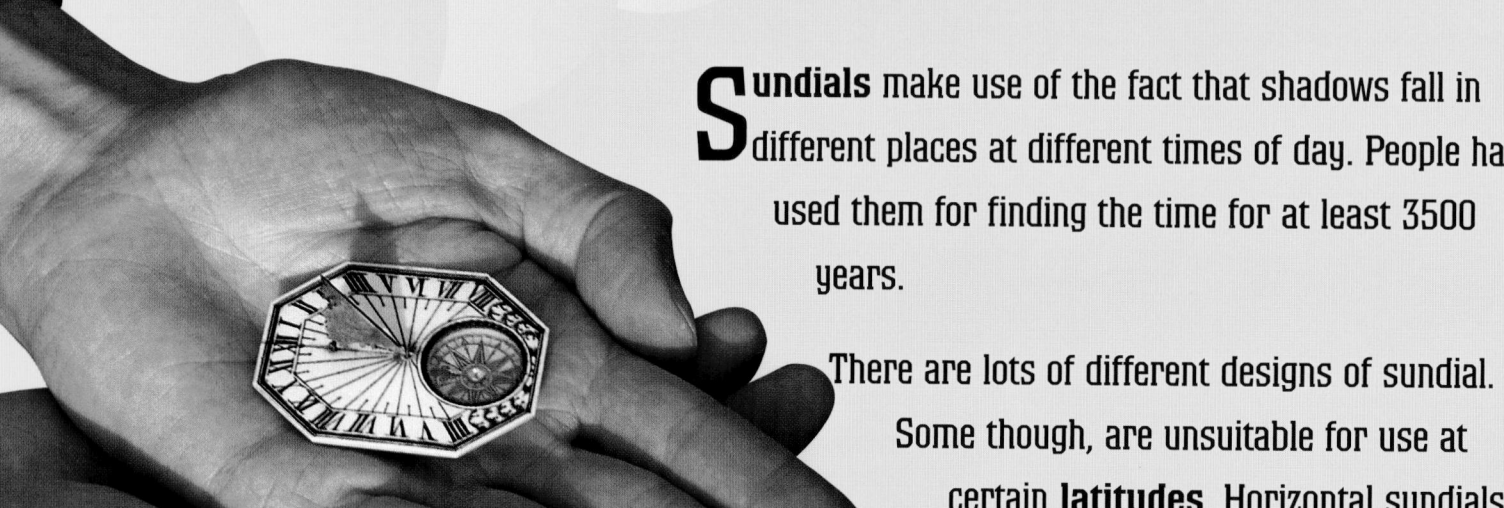

Sundials make use of the fact that shadows fall in different places at different times of day. People have used them for finding the time for at least 3500 years.

There are lots of different designs of sundial. Some though, are unsuitable for use at certain **latitudes**. Horizontal sundials, for example, are often seen in the British Isles, the United States and Australia, but not near the **Equator**.

Portable sundials like this were used from about the mid sixteenth century until the first half of the nineteenth century, when accurate watches became more widely available. This French one is over 300 years old.

Hours of unequal length

Many of the oldest surviving sundials have been marked to divide the period of daylight into 12 hours. Until the fourteenth century, this was how the day in many countries had come to be divided up. It meant that the length of each daylight hour and each night-time hour varied with the seasons, with daytime hours being longer in the summer than in the winter.

Hours of equal length

It was the invention of the mechanical clock that eventually led to our days being divided into hours of equal length. Hours recorded by most clocks, always consist of the same number of evenly spaced ticks, and so are always the same length.

In the past, vertical sundials were the most common type. They were fixed on the outside walls of buildings, at a height where they couldn't be easily touched. The spacing of the hour marks depends on both the sundial's latitude and the direction that the wall is facing.

As more and more clocks came to be built, so more and more sundials came to be marked to show equal hours too. Until the twentieth century, most people had to rely on a sundial for setting their clocks and watches to the right time.

This horizontal sundial was made in 1582 for use in a garden in the northern hemisphere. The numbers are marked in a clockwise direction. If it had been made for use in the southern hemisphere, the tip of the gnomon would point towards the south and the numbers would be marked in an anticlockwise direction.

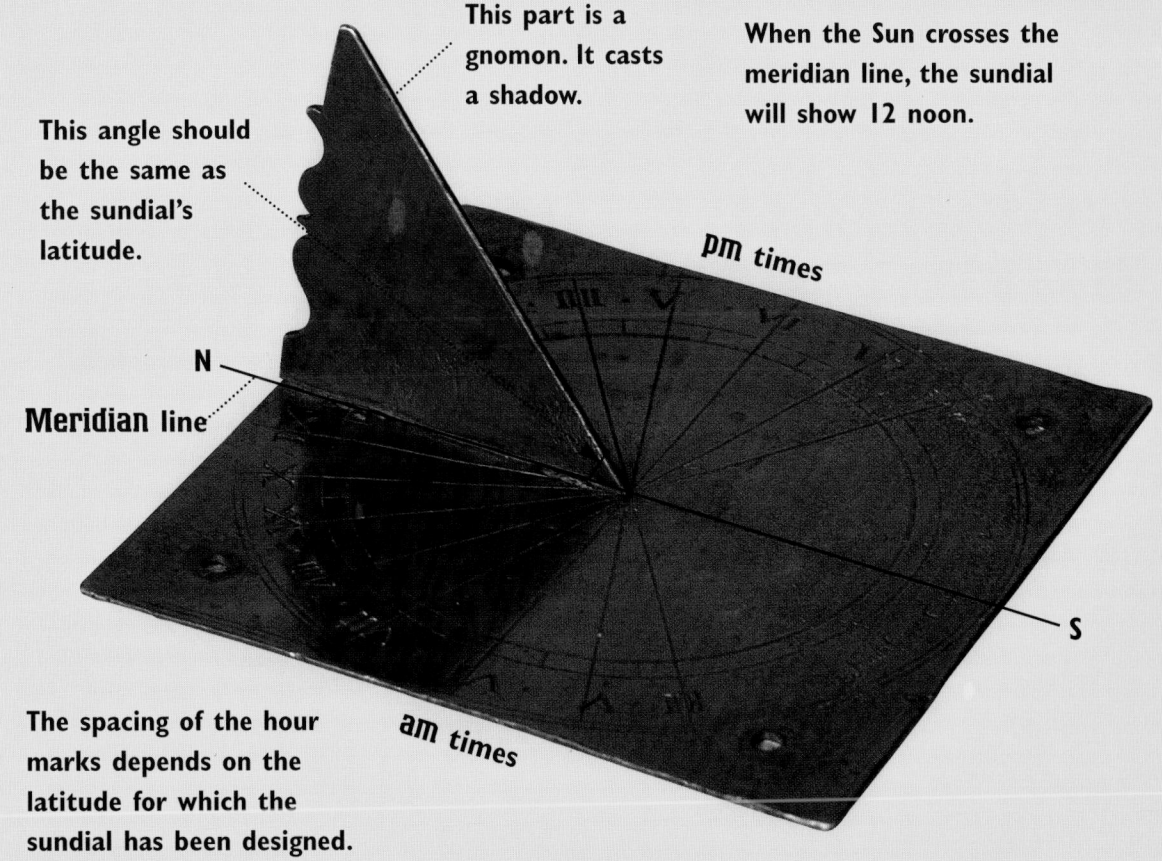

This part is a gnomon. It casts a shadow.

This angle should be the same as the sundial's latitude.

When the Sun crosses the meridian line, the sundial will show 12 noon.

pm times

N

Meridian line

S

am times

The spacing of the hour marks depends on the latitude for which the sundial has been designed.

The First Clocks

One of the problems with a **sundial** (a time finder), is that it can't tell you the time at night when the Sun is not shining. Even in the sunniest places, sundials can't be used for long stretches of time. The solution lay in building timekeepers – devices which would allow people to keep track of the time when they were unable to find it directly from the Sun or the stars.

A copy of a water clock that was in use in a temple in Egypt about 3400 years ago. Inside, there are different scales for different times of the year. This is because the length of each 'Egyptian hour' varied with the seasons.

Water clocks

One of the earliest timekeepers was a container full of water with a hole in the bottom. Water clocks were used in the monasteries of Europe for many hundreds of years. They were used to ensure that the bells which were rung to wake the monks and call them to prayer throughout the day were rung at the right time.

This modern model shows part of a giant water clock which was completed in China in 1092. The waterwheel turned with a series of stop-start movements or 'ticks'.

The first mechanical clocks

It was probably in the monasteries that the first mechanical clocks were built. Although no one knows quite when or where they were invented, several monasteries and cathedrals appear to have had one by the end of the thirteenth century.

The first mechanical clocks were big and heavy. They contained metal cogs (which were turned by a weight) and a bell. They also contained a mechanism called an **escapement** which controlled the rate at which the cogs turned.

The clocks were poor timekeepers. At best, they could keep the right time to within about a quarter of an hour each day. Unlike modern clocks, they had no face or hands. They told the time by ringing a bell every hour. The first clocks to have hands normally only had an hour hand fitted. Minute hands only started to become common in the mid seventeenth century, when the accuracy of clocks improved with the introduction of the **pendulum**.

The escape wheel turns by one tooth's worth for every 'there and back' swing of the foliot. As it turns, other cogs in the clock (which are not shown in the diagram) turn slightly too.

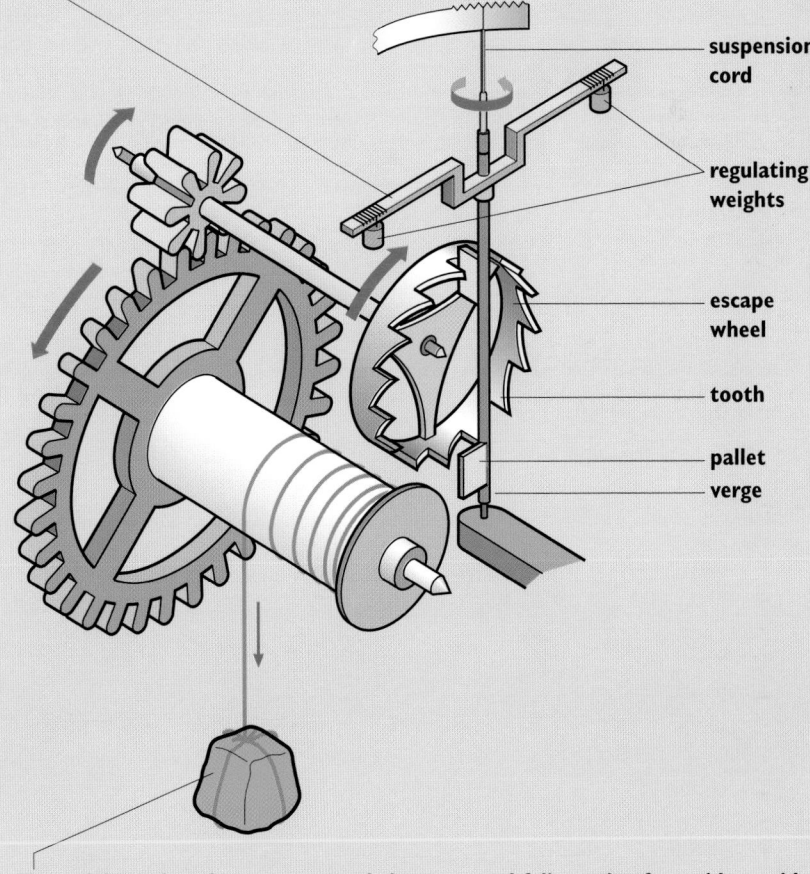

The foliot swings from side to side and controls the rate at which the clock ticks.

suspension cord

regulating weights

escape wheel

tooth

pallet

verge

The weight makes the cogs turn and the verge and foliot swing from side to side.

13

Interval Timers

A candle can be used as an interval timer. If it is to be used as a timekeeper, the time when it is lit must be known.

Fire, sand and water

Although **sundials** could be used for telling the time of day when it was sunny, they couldn't be used inside a building or for measuring short intervals of time. The first mechanical clocks weren't much use for measuring short time intervals either.

Over the years, many different types of interval timers have been designed. Many made use of sand, fire or water – some of them are shown here. A good timer is one that is easy to use, and always gives the same results.

This water timer was made in about 1670. It works in a similar way to a sandglass. When turned, the decorative cap is removed and the water takes 30 minutes to run from the top to the bottom.

In this Chinese fire clock, a stick of burning incense burns through the threads one by one, allowing the weights to fall onto a metal tray with a clang.

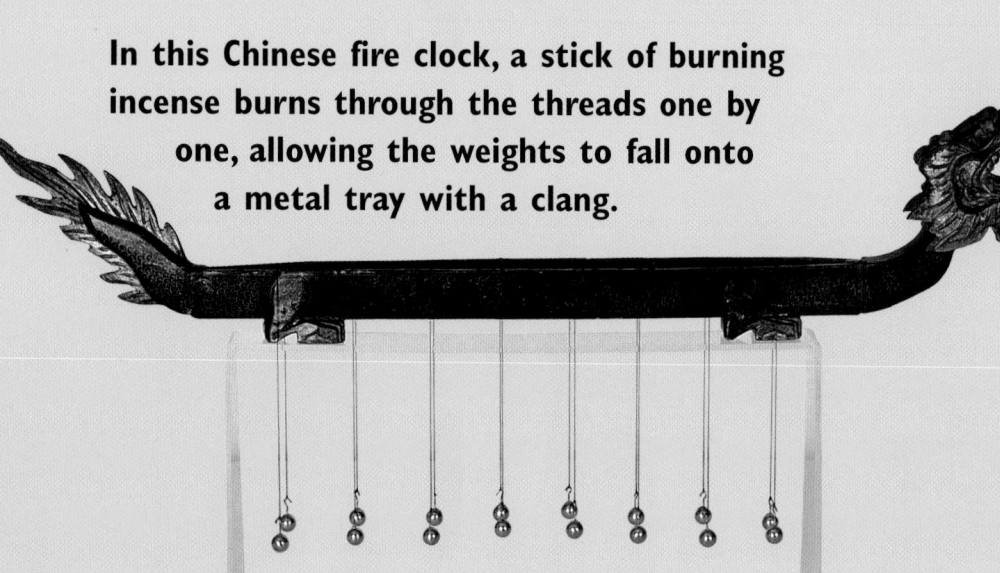

Sandglasses

Sandglasses were invented in the fourteenth century. They were used in many different places. These included the law courts and churches, where they were used to make sure that people did not speak for too long.

Doctors used them to measure pulse rates, whilst sailors used them to estimate their speed (by measuring how far they had gone in a particular time). Sailors also used them to time the watches (the period when a particular sailor was on duty). Sailors keeping watch at night would sometimes 'flog the glass' – in other words, would turn it early, so that they could finish their watch early too! Sand timers were also used by cooks, and can still be bought today.

A teacher using a sandglass in the fourteenth century.

This sandglass is over 350 years old. The sand takes one hour to run from the top container to the bottom one.

This modern sandglass was designed for classroom use. The sand takes one minute to run from the top container to the bottom one.

15

Better Timekeepers
and Portable Timekeepers

pendulum

weight

This clock was built in the 1660s. Like many other old clocks, it has been modified, and no longer has its original escapement.

Clocks use energy

Clocks need a source of energy to make their cogs and hands turn, and their bells ring. In the earliest clocks, the energy came from a slowly falling weight. Even when such clocks got smaller and lighter, the weight prevented them from being moved while they were still running. It also prevented them from being placed for example on top of a table or a cupboard.

In the late fifteenth century, clockmakers started to use the energy stored in a coiled spring to drive some of their clocks. Unlike weight-driven clocks, spring-driven ones could be positioned almost anywhere.

Pendulum clocks

A **pendulum** will swing from side to side at a steadier rate than the **foliot** used in the earliest clocks. The first proper pendulum clock was designed by Christiaan Huygens in 1656. Built by Salomon Coster, it was completed in 1657. It was far more accurate than any timekeeper that had been built before.

Clocks which were designed to be moved frequently had big handles on the tops of their cases. The carrying case alongside this spring-driven clock is covered with leather.

The anchor escapement shown here was an improvement on the verge escapement used by Huygens in the first pendulum clock. As the pendulum swings from side to side, the escape wheel is allowed to turn in a series of steps or ticks. As it turns, the hands and other cogs in the clock (not shown here) turn slightly too.

anchor escapement

escape wheel

driving weight

pendulum

Unlike most earlier clocks, it was fitted with both a minute hand and an hour hand. Over the years the accuracy of the best available pendulum clocks improved from roughly 10 seconds a day to one second a year.

This French watch is about 350 years old. Like most other clocks and watches of its age, it was made without a minute hand. The chain is called a chatelaine. The winding key and two seals (for sealing letters) are attached to it.

Wrist-watches

The first wrist-watches appeared in the late 1800s, becoming much more common during the First World War. Most watches made until the 1970s, were spring-driven and regulated by the **oscillations** of a **balance wheel** and balance spring. Most modern watches are electrically driven (by a battery), and regulated by the oscillations taking place inside a **quartz** crystal.

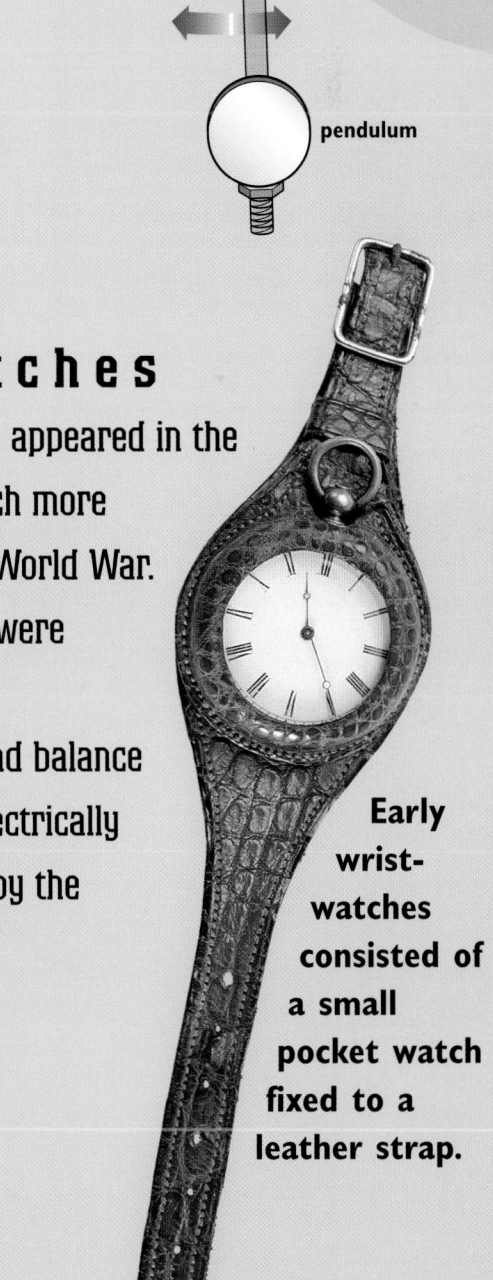

Early wrist-watches consisted of a small pocket watch fixed to a leather strap.

Finding Time

One turn later: The Earth needs to rotate through about 1° more to bring the person back to midday (square on to the Sun).

The Earth turns through about 361° from one midday to the next. This means that it rotates on its axis 366¼ times during the course of a 365¼ day year.

Between **midday** today and midday tomorrow, (when the Sun crosses the same **meridian**) our Earth will have turned on its **axis** through an angle of about 361 degrees (361°). The Earth has to turn through about one degree more than one full turn (360°) to take us from one midday to the next because it is also moving around the Sun.

Some days are longer than others!

The Earth's **orbit** is slightly elliptical (oval in shape). The Earth is closest to the Sun in January, and furthest from it in July. As the Earth gets closer to the Sun, it travels more quickly in its orbit – and when this happens, it has to turn a very tiny amount further on its axis from one midday to the next. This means that each natural or **solar day** varies slightly in length throughout the year.

Sidereal days are always the same length

Unlike the Sun, a star will cross the same meridian line each time the Earth spins exactly once on its axis. By observing the stars with a telescope pointing along the meridian, astronomers are able to record the moment that each star crosses from one side to the other more accurately. The time taken for the Earth to turn through 360° on its axis is always the same and is known as a **sidereal day**. A sidereal day is approximately 4 minutes shorter than the average length of a solar day or **mean solar day**.

The telescope can be moved up and down, but not from side to side. Each turn of the Earth brings the same star back into view. Telescopes like this are called **transit telescopes**. Most observatories had one in the late seventeenth century. One of their uses was to check the accuracy of the observatory's main sidereal clock. The sidereal clock was then used to check other clocks. All the clocks could be checked, because mean solar time can be calculated from sidereal time.

Finding the time with a telescope

Because individual stars always cross a particular meridian at the same sidereal time each day, their regular observation allows the time to be found far more accurately than can be done with a **sundial** or from observations of the Sun. The telescope is a bit like a clock hand (sweeping across the sky as the Earth spins on its axis), whilst the stars are a bit like the numbers on a dial. **Observatories** had some clocks set to show mean solar time (which is what ordinary people's clocks would have shown) and others that looked the same but ticked slightly faster, which were set to show sidereal time.

This transit telescope was the ultimate source of Greenwich Mean Time from 1816 to 1850.

Local Time
and Greenwich Mean Time

Local apparent time

The further west you are, the later the Sun rises, and the later it sets. When a **sundial** in London says 12.00, one to the west in Plymouth will only say 11.44. The time shown by a sundial is the **local apparent time**.

Mean time

At the start of the nineteenth century, anyone lucky enough to own a clock or a watch, would probably have set it to their own **local time**. It would have shown local mean solar time, more commonly known as local **mean time**. Local mean time is sometimes ahead of local apparent time and sometimes behind it. The local mean time at Greenwich is called **Greenwich Mean Time**. It is 16 minutes ahead of Plymouth Mean Time.

This pocket-watch was made in the mid 1800s. It has two minute hands. One would have been set to Greenwich Mean Time and the other to the user's own local time.

Standard time

In the days before the railways, when local time was still in common use, a journey from London to Plymouth would probably have taken several days. Each time travellers stopped at an inn, they would reset their watches to a slightly earlier time. By the time they reached Plymouth, their watches would be set 16 minutes earlier than the clocks in London.

The railways allowed journeys like these to be made far more quickly by far more people. Imagine three passengers on a train to Plymouth: one who had got on at London, one who had got on at Reading, and one who had got on at Exeter. If each of the passengers had a watch set to their own local time, what would each say when the train arrived at Plymouth at 3.00 in the afternoon **local time**? The London passenger's watch would say 3.16, the Reading passenger's 3.12, and the Exeter passenger's 3.02. You can probably imagine how confusing things could get, especially when it came to working out the timetables!

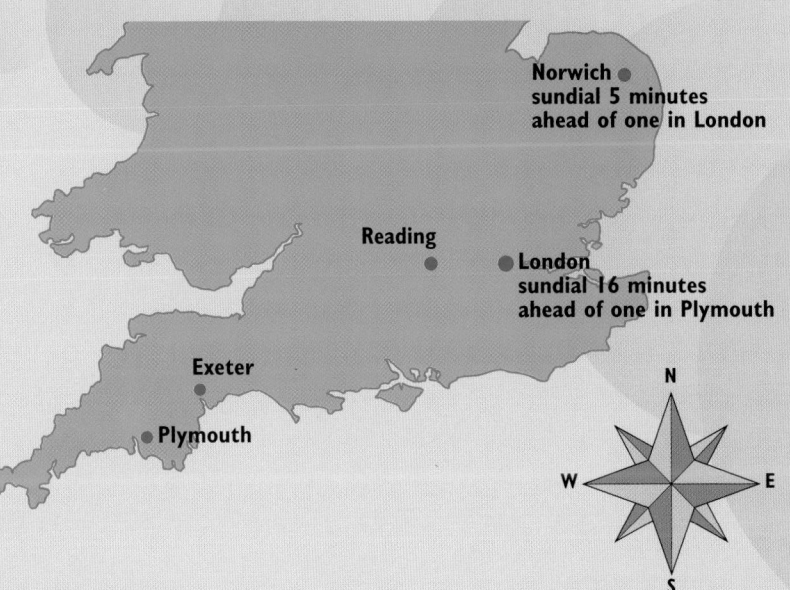

Norwich ●
sundial 5 minutes
ahead of one in London

Reading ●

● London
sundial 16 minutes
ahead of one in Plymouth

Exeter ●

● Plymouth

N

W   E

S

A sundial (or clock set to local time) in London will show an earlier time than one in Norwich to the east, but a later time than one in Plymouth to the west.

The British railway companies solved the problem by using Greenwich Mean Time (rather than local time) at all their stations. Years later, in 1880, the British Government decided that, since most people were already using it, Greenwich Mean Time should become the **standard time** used by everyone in the British Isles.

The railway companies in other countries faced similar and sometimes greater problems. In America, where the difference in local time between New York City on the East Coast and San Francisco on the West is over three and a quarter hours, the final solution came in 1883 when five different **time zones** each with its own standard time were set up.

What's the Time?

The time-ball at the Greenwich Observatory was installed in 1833. The ball drops from the top of the mast at 1 o'clock in the afternoon each day. It was used by sailors on the nearby River Thames to set their **chronometers** before starting out across the oceans.

Time signals

When we want to know the time, we normally look at a watch or a clock. You may have noticed though, that different people's watches often say slightly different times. So how do we know what the time really is? One way we can find out is from the television or radio. Most radio presenters tell their listeners the time at frequent intervals. They usually say something like 'The time is now twenty-eight minutes past eight'. The trouble is, this takes a few seconds to say and you the listener can't be sure of exactly when it was twenty-eight minutes past eight. Was it as the presenter started to speak, when they finished, or somewhere in between?

As a result of this, some radio stations transmit a special time signal. At certain times of the day, usually on the hour, a small number of pips are broadcast in quick succession. The first pips are a warning to get ready and the last pip is the one to set your watch by. In France these time signals consist of three pips, but in the UK they consist of six. The first British time signal ever to be transmitted came from the Royal **Observatory** at Greenwich – the home of **Greenwich Mean Time**. Some modern clocks contain a radio receiver and automatically adjust themselves to the correct time.

The speaking clock

You could try telephoning a speaking clock instead. The first speaking clock was set up in France in 1905. The British speaking clock was set up in 1936. It gives the time every 10 seconds.

What happened before time signals?

Before television and radio, it was much harder for people to check their clocks and watches. Most people had to rely on a **sundial**, or another clock that had been checked with a sundial.

The time-ball at the Sydney Observatory in Australia was installed in 1858. The mechanism was made in London.

This clock outside the Greenwich Observatory was installed for public use in 1852. The hour hand goes round once each day – so the time shown is a few seconds before 9.07 am. The clock is controlled by a master clock, which sends electrical signals once each second to make it tick at the correct rate. People still use it to check their watches.

23

Longitude and Time

Latitude and longitude

Lines of **latitude** mark how far north or south you are. Lines of **longitude** mark how far east or west you are. Unlike latitude, which is measured from the **Equator**, there is no obvious point from which to measure longitude. Until 1884, it was measured from many different places, including Greenwich, Paris and Lisbon. After 1884, there was officially only one place – the **meridian** line running through the Royal **Observatory** at Greenwich.

Where am I?

When Christopher Columbus sailed across the Atlantic Ocean in 1492, there was no way of measuring a ship's longitude once it was out of sight of land. Much of the world remained unexplored and the sea **charts** (maps) were inaccurate and incomplete. In later years, as the trade routes opened up, these problems became more and more important. Journeys often took longer than expected, and could end in disaster if a ship got lost and then ran aground. As a result, large rewards were offered to anyone who could find a way of measuring longitude at sea. The two solutions when they came, were both linked to the measurement of time.

Shipwrecks would often result in the loss of life and cargo as well as the loss of the ship.

Longitude is linked to time

When it is **midday** on one side of the Earth, it is midnight on the other. Each 15 degrees (15°) of longitude is equivalent to a time difference of one hour. So to find how far east or west they had sailed, all sailors had to do was to find out both the **local time** (which could be done from observations of the positions of the Sun or the stars) and the time back home at exactly the same moment.

Finding the time back home

How though was a sailor supposed to find out what the time was back home? One suggestion was to take to sea a clock set to show it. However, clocks in 1600 were not accurate enough to be reliable at sea, and the more accurate **pendulum** clocks, invented in 1656, would not work because the pendulum would swing at different speeds due to the rocking of the boat. Throughout the sixteenth and seventeenth centuries, most people thought that a sufficiently accurate seagoing clock could never be built and looked for solutions elsewhere.

The latitude of this ship is 27° north, its longitude is 74° west. Its latitude could have been found either from measurements of the height of the midday Sun or from the height of the Pole Star. The time difference (local time) from Greenwich is 4 hours 56 minutes.

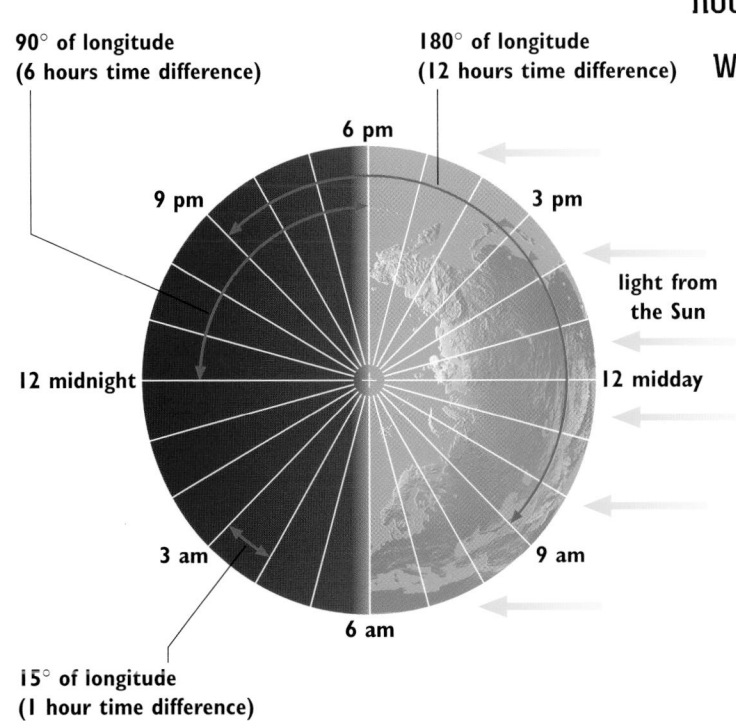

Longitude and time.

The Nautical Almanac –
One Solution to the Longitude Problem

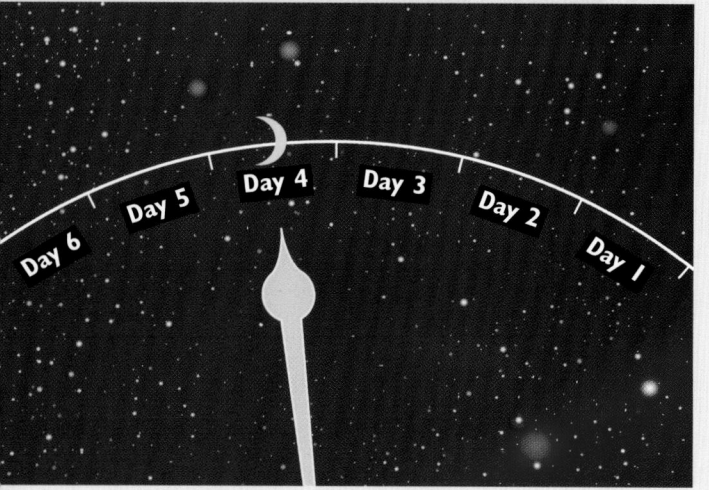

Tick-tock Moon clock

Longitude can be measured with the help of the Moon. At the same time as the Earth is rotating on its **axis**, the Moon is **orbiting** it in the same direction. This makes the Moon appear to move across the sky from east to west at a slightly slower rate than the stars. As the night goes on, the Moon slowly moves across the background of stars; rather like a hand moving across the face of a clock.

The Moon appears to move against the background of stars and can be used as a clock to find the time at Greenwich. The Moon (the hand) takes 27½ days to go around the dial (the stars) once. Sailors were only able to read the Moon clock with the help of the Nautical Almanac.

Unfortunately, the Moon clock can only be read with the help of tables listing where the Moon will be seen at different times on different days of the year. The Royal **Observatory** at Greenwich produced the first set of tables for use by sailors in 1766. They listed where the Moon would be seen at different times from Greenwich for the following three years. The book containing the tables was called the **Nautical Almanac**.

A page from the first Nautical Almanac. The almanac was produced with the help of lunar tables provided by the German astronomer Tobias Mayer.

Using the Nautical Almanac

Sailors wanting to know their longitude had to measure three angles – the angle up to the Moon, the angle up to a nearby bright star, and the angle between them. After several long calculations, they would then be able to read off the time at Greenwich from the Nautical Almanac. Provided the sailors had also found their own **local time**, they would then be able to calculate the time difference from Greenwich. All that had to be done then was to turn the time difference into a longitude difference – each hour of time representing 15 degrees (15°) of longitude.

This method of measuring longitude is called the lunar distance method. It turned out to be very reliable, and was used by many ocean-going sailors from around 1780 until well into the 1800s. It was the publication of the first Nautical Almanac that started the chain of events that led to Greenwich becoming the home of the **Prime Meridian** and the centre of time in 1884.

Having measured these three angles, a sailor could then use the Nautical Almanac to find the time at Greenwich, and hence his longitude.

A room at the Greenwich Observatory in 1676. The Observatory was founded by King Charles II of England to help solve the longitude problem. The two clocks to the left of the door were used to check that the Earth spins on its axis at a steady rate.

Harrison's Seagoing Clocks –
A Second Solution to the Longitude Problem

The fabulous longitude prize

In 1714, the British Government set up the Board of **Longitude**. The Board of Longitude offered a reward or prize of up to £20,000 to anyone who could find a means of measuring longitude to the nearest half a degree. In today's terms, this would make you as rich as winning the lottery!

Could a clock win?

John Harrison, a carpenter and self-taught clockmaker got to hear of the prize, and decided that he would try to win it. He knew that to win the prize any clock that he built would

H1

have to gain or lose no more than 2.8 seconds a day whilst at sea. He designed a completely new type of clock without a **pendulum**, so that it wouldn't be affected by the tossing of a boat. The clock is now known as H1. When it was tested at sea in 1736, it performed far better than any clock that had ever been to sea before – but it wasn't good enough to win the longitude prize.

H2

John Harrison finally wins the prize

Harrison was offered £500 to develop a modified design. By the time H2 was finished two years later, Harrison realized that this clock too would not win the prize.

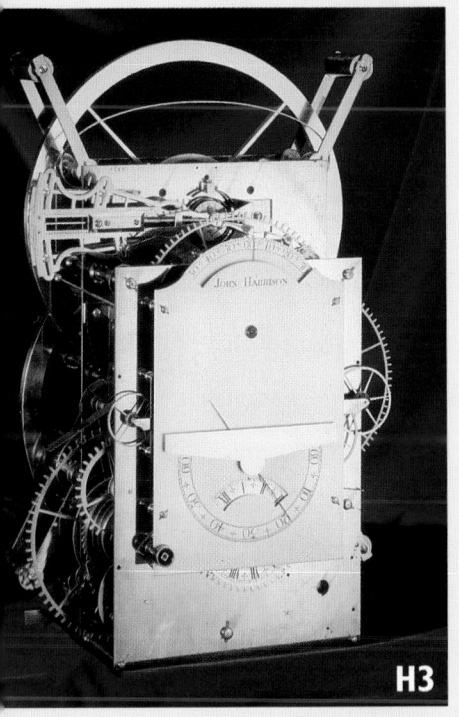

H3

Without even having it tested at sea, he set to work on a third clock (H3). He worked on H3 for the next 19 years, but knew in the end that it would not work well enough. Whilst still working on H3, Harrison decided to try out a different design. H4, the clock that he built, looks from the outside rather like a giant pocket-watch. It was tested at sea in 1761.

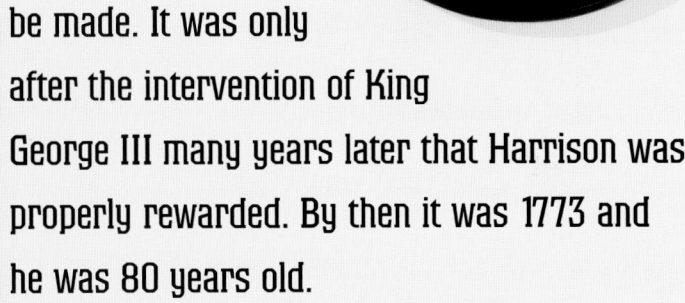

H4

Although Harrison thought that H4 had performed well enough to win the £20,000 prize, the Board of Longitude weren't happy with the fairness of the test and refused to award him the full prize. They demanded that further tests be carried out and that copies of H4 be made. It was only after the intervention of King George III many years later that Harrison was properly rewarded. By then it was 1773 and he was 80 years old.

A copy of H4 was taken by Captain Cook on his second voyage of discovery to the Pacific in 1772. He described it as 'our never failing guide', and used it to construct some of the first **charts** of Australia and New Zealand. Many people now consider H4 to be the most important clock ever to have been made. It was to lead to the development of both more accurate watches, and other seagoing clocks or **chronometers**.

John Harrison. H4 is on the table, with H3 behind it. H3 is similar in size to H1 and H2.

The Prime Meridian
and the Universal Day

In the early 1880s, sailors measured east and west from several different places. The main meridians used are shown here.

East and west from where?

The end of the 1760s marked a turning-point in navigation. After years of being unable to measure their **longitude** at sea, sailors now had two ways of measuring it. Both worked by measuring time differences. Although a **chronometer** (a seagoing clock) would allow the difference in time from any chosen town or city to be measured directly, this was not the case with the lunar distance method. The **Nautical Almanac** gave only the time on the **meridian** that ran through the Royal **Observatory** at Greenwich. Not everyone chose to measure longitude at sea from the Greenwich meridian. The French and Algerians for example, measured it from the Paris meridian, whilst the Swedes measured it from the Stockholm meridian.

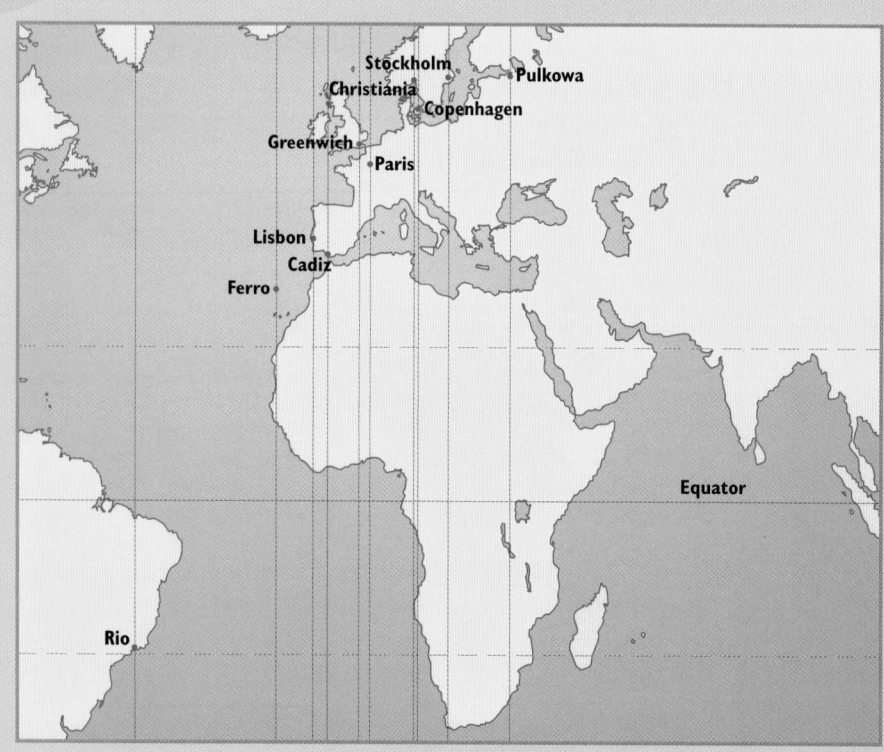

Choosing a Prime Meridian

By the early 1880s, many countries could see the advantages of measuring east and west from just one single meridian. As a result, the International Meridian Conference took place in Washington, USA in 1884. The meridian line running through the eyepiece of the transit telescope then in use at Greenwich was chosen as the **Prime Meridian** of the world. There were several reasons why the Greenwich meridian was chosen – the main one being that nearly two-thirds of the world's ships were already using it.

Universal Time and the Universal Day

The conference also decided to create a single time system for the whole world. Up until then, time had always been measured from different starting points according to whereabouts in the world you were. For example, the day in London started after the day in Sydney, but before the day in New York. The Universal Day gave people an easy way of measuring time from the same starting point, no matter where on the Earth's surface they were.

The Prime Meridian starts in the eyepiece of this transit telescope at the Royal Observatory in Greenwich. The telescope was the source of Greenwich Mean Time from 1851 until 1927.

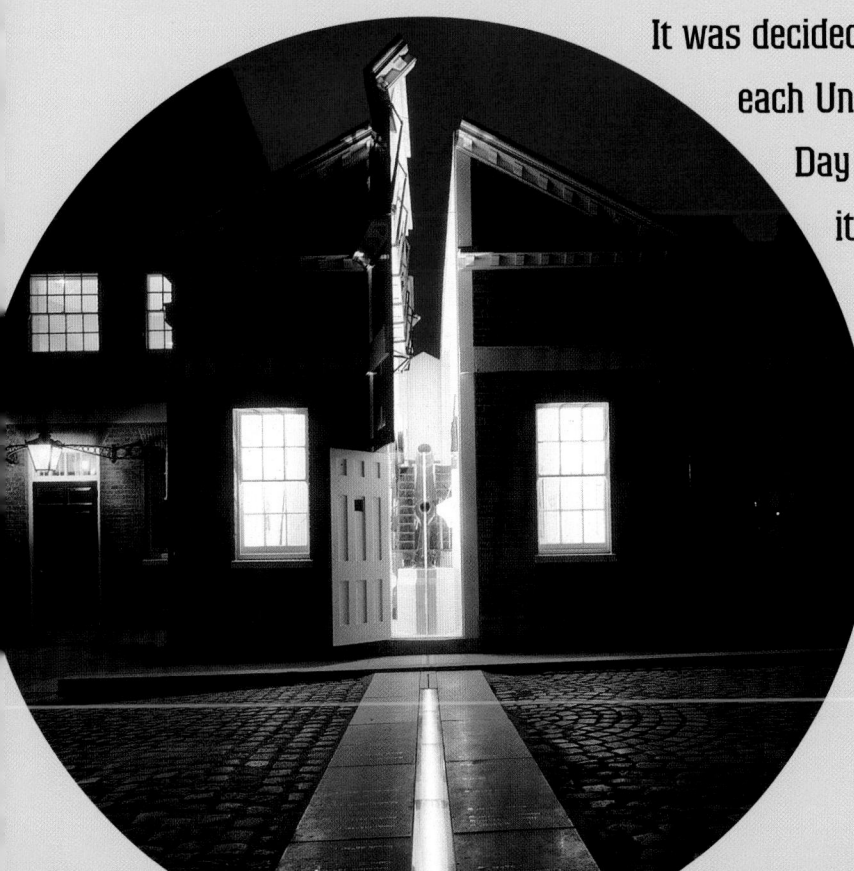

It was decided that each Universal Day would start for the whole world at the moment it reached midnight on the Greenwich meridian. **Greenwich Mean Time** therefore became the 'official' time for the world. Since 1928, it has also been known as **Universal Time** (UT). Following the International Meridian Conference, agreement was reached for setting up our present system of **time zones**.

The Prime Meridian outside the observatory buildings at Greenwich.

Time Zones

Greenwich – the centre of time

Following the International **Meridian** Conference of 1884, more and more countries started to use **standard time** rather than **local time**. Some large countries, for example Australia and Russia, were divided into several **time zones**. Other large countries, such as China and India, used the same standard time for the whole country.

The **Prime Meridian** and **Greenwich Mean Time** became the centre of the time zone system. Countries to the east normally used standard times a whole number of hours ahead of Greenwich Mean Time, whilst those to the west normally used standard times that were a whole number of hours behind.

The world's countries fit loosely into a grid of 24 time zones – each 15 degrees of longitude 'wide'.

Greenwich
Prime Meridian
New York
Lagos
Rio de Janeiro

Summer time

Some countries, for example the UK and France, switch to **summer time** (daylight saving time) for part of the year. They do this by putting the clocks forward by an hour in the spring, and putting them back again in the autumn.

The switch is made in order to make better use of the daylight hours – so for example, instead of getting light at 5 o'clock in the morning (while you are probably still in bed) and dark at 7 o'clock in the evening, it gets light at 6 o'clock in the morning and dark at 8 o'clock in the evening.

In the UK British Summer Time (BST) is kept between the last Sunday in March and the last Sunday in October.

The International Date Line

The *Victoria* was the first ship to sail round the world. It set off from Europe in a westerly direction on 20 September 1519. Just before it reached home, it stopped off for supplies at the Cape Verde Islands. The crew were surprised to find that it was Thursday 10 July 1522. They thought the date was Wednesday 9 July 1522.

Something similar would happen to you if you were to set off around the world in a westerly direction and turn your watch back by an hour each time you entered a new time zone. By the time you got back home, your watch would show a time which was 24 hours behind everybody else's!

To prevent things like this from happening to travellers, an imaginary line known as the **International Date Line** has been created on the opposite side of the world to Greenwich. When people cross the date line, they have to adjust the date shown by their watches. The direction in which the adjustment is made depends on whether they are travelling from east to west or from west to east.

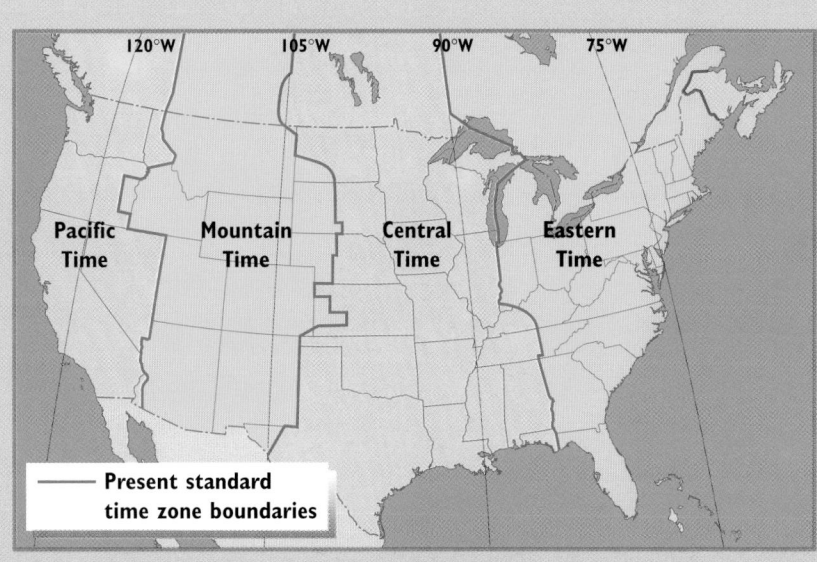

North America's time zones.

Our Slowing Earth

Our Earth is slowing down! By the early 1900s timekeepers had so improved that they enabled astronomers to detect and measure slight changes in the rate at which the Earth is spinning. They found that the Earth was continually speeding up and slowing down and that, in the long run, the Earth was getting slower.

By studying the daily growth bands of fossil corals (which vary with the seasons), scientists have discovered that 400 million years ago, there were more days in a year, and that the Earth took only 22 of our present hours to spin round once on its axis.

The elastic second

Although the changes were far too small to bother most people, they did start to bother astronomers and scientists. If the rate at which the Earth was spinning kept changing, then the exact length of a second would keep changing too! Eventually in 1956, astronomers and scientists fixed the length of a second. The length they chose was equal to the average length the second had had in the year 1900.

The fixed second

In the meantime, a group of scientists had been developing **atomic clocks**. They were many thousands of times more accurate than the best **pendulum** clocks. So in 1967, without changing the length of a second, scientists changed its definition to one based on **atomic time**.

Without any adjustment, the time shown by atomic clocks would eventually get more and more out of step with the movement of the

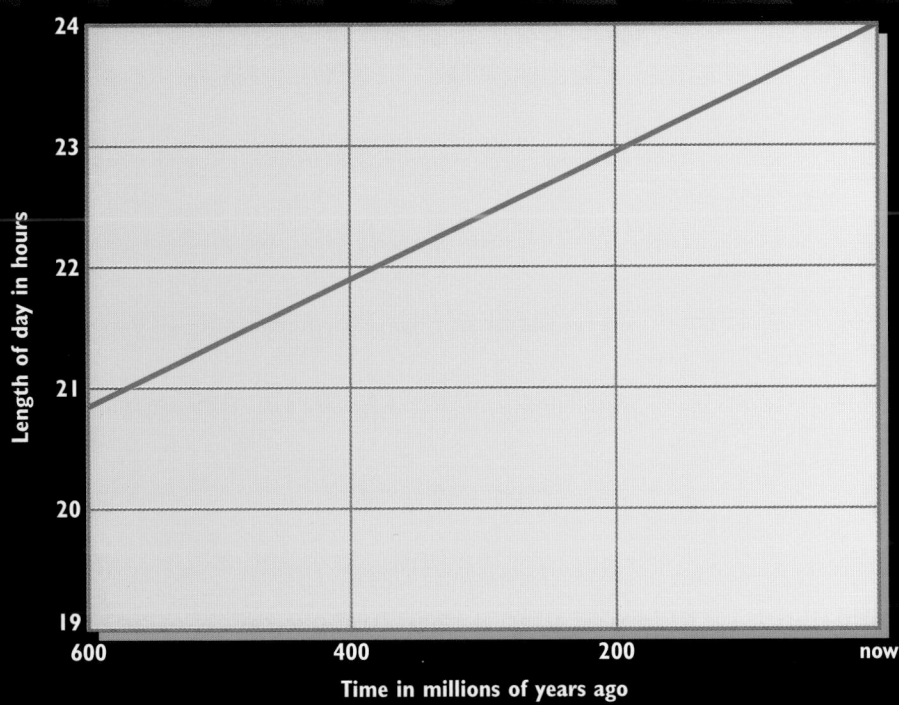

Length of day in hours

24
23
22
21
20
19

600   400   200   now

Time in millions of years ago

Our days are gradually getting longer.

Sun across the sky. This is because the clocks would carry on ticking at a steady rate even though the Earth was slowing down. In a few thousand years time, unadjusted atomic clocks could end up saying that it was 12.00 and lunchtime, even though people were only just getting up in the morning! To prevent this from happening, our present system of adding or subtracting **leap seconds** was started.

Co-ordinated Universal Time

Atomic time which has been adjusted by the addition or subtraction of leap seconds is called **Co-ordinated Universal Time** (UTC). The time shown by most clocks around the world today is based on it. The adjustments are made so that Co-ordinated Universal Time never differs from **Greenwich Mean Time** by more than 0.9 seconds. Between 1972 and the start of 1999, a total of 22 leap seconds were added. Whenever a leap second is added, the British time signal on the radio consists of seven pips rather than the normal six. Leap seconds are normally only added or subtracted at the very end (midnight UTC) of the last day of June, or the last day of December.

In the UK most people still say their clocks are set to Greenwich Mean Time – even though they have set them to Co-ordinated Universal Time.

Timekeepers
more Accurate than the Earth

A tiny computer chip inside the watch makes the quartz crystal vibrate. It also counts the vibrations and as a result, produces one electrical impulse each second. This is fed to a motor that turns the hands.

battery

The slice of quartz crystal is enclosed inside this protective casing.

Clocks count oscillations

Clocks work by counting vibrations or **oscillations** – for example the swings of a **pendulum**. The minute hand of a clock with a pendulum that takes one second to swing from side to side, will turn through one-tenth of a degree with every swing, and through 360 degrees with every 3600 swings. The clock will count 86,400 swings of the pendulum each day, and 604,800 swings each week.

Quartz clocks

In the same way that an oscillating pendulum was found to swing more regularly than the oscillating **foliot** used in the earliest clocks, a slice of vibrating **quartz** crystal oscillates more regularly than a pendulum. The tiny piece of quartz crystal buried inside a clock or watch vibrates or oscillates tens of thousands of times each second – a rate so fast that to the naked eye it wouldn't appear to be vibrating at all.

If you have a quartz watch or clock, it almost certainly keeps time to better than one second a day – something that only **chronometers** and the most expensive pendulum clocks could do at the end of the nineteenth century. Specially engineered quartz clocks are able to keep time thousands of times more accurately than the ones you have at home.

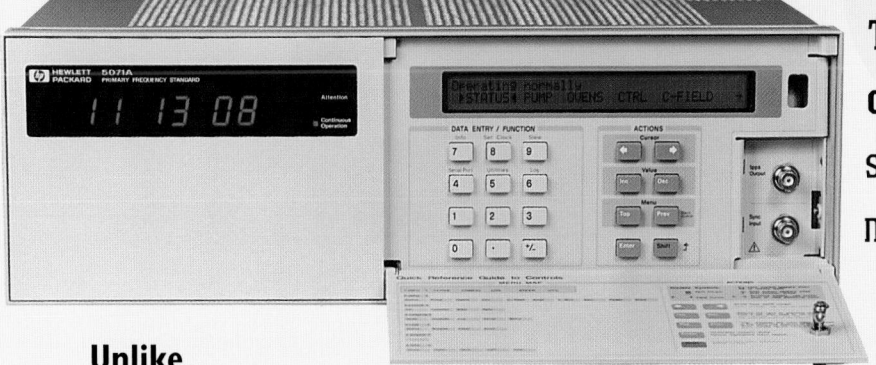

Atomic clocks

The world's most accurate clocks are **atomic clocks**. They make use of microwaves similar to those used by mobile phones and microwave ovens. The microwaves are produced inside the clock by an oscillator vibrating 9,192,631,770 times a second.

Unlike timekeeper Earth which at the moment is losing around 1 second a year, this atomic clock would lose or gain no more than a second in the next 1,600,000 years (if it could be kept going for that long)! Our time today comes from the averaged readings of over 200 atomic clocks distributed around the world.

When a beam of **caesium** atoms is bombarded with the microwaves, the atoms absorb the wave energy, and change their magnetic properties. The caesium atoms are used to help adjust the rate of the oscillator to exactly 9,192,631,770 vibrations a second, as they will only absorb microwaves at this frequency. An electronic device then counts the vibrations and converts the count rate into a time on a clock face.

In 1967, scientists redefined the second as the period equal to the duration of 9,192,631,770 of these vibrations – so every time 9,192,631,770 vibrations are counted, the time shown by the digital display increases by one second!

Modern communication systems depend on the split-second timing provided by atomic clocks.

Months and Years

We see the Moon, because it reflects light from the Sun. The side of the Moon that is facing the Sun is always lit up. When the Moon is at A, between the Earth and the Sun, all the lit side is facing away from the Earth, and none of the Moon can be seen – a new moon. Roughly two weeks later, when the Moon is on the opposite side of the Earth at E, all the lit face can be seen – a full moon.

The phases of the Moon

The appearance of the Moon changes in a regular pattern as it **orbits** the Earth. It was around these changes or phases that many of our ancestors constructed their calendars. The length of our months is based on the length of time between one new moon and the next. A new moon occurs when the Moon passes in its orbit between the Earth and the Sun.

Synodic months

At the same time as the Moon is going around the Earth, the Earth is also going around the Sun. The Moon therefore has to complete slightly more than one full orbit of the Earth from one new moon to the next. It takes just over 29½ days for it to do this. This length of time is known as a **synodic month**. In the time that the Earth takes to orbit the Sun once, there are twelve synodic months with roughly eleven extra days left over.

Position	Appearance of Moon	
	view from near the North Pole	view from near the South Pole
A new moon	Moon not visible	Moon not visible
B		
C first quarter		
D		
E full moon		
F		
G last quarter		
H		

Light from the Sun

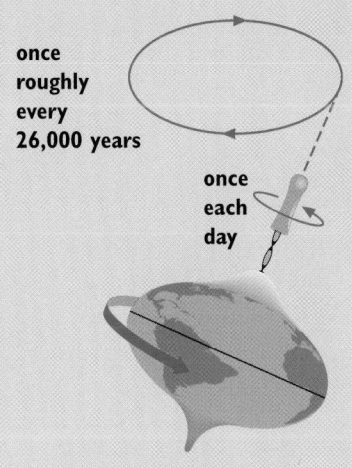

once
roughly
every
26,000 years

once
each
day

The Earth spinning on its axis is a bit like a spinning top, whose handle traces out a circle as it spins. This is called **precession**. It takes about 26,000 years for the Earth's axis or 'handle' to trace out one full circle. Compared to today, in about 13,000 years time, the Earth's axis will be leaning in completely the opposite direction.

The tropical year

As the Earth orbits the Sun, although the direction in which its **axis** is leaning hardly changes from year to year, the change starts to get very noticeable over a period of hundreds or thousands of years. To ensure that winter in the northern hemisphere always starts in December, the **Gregorian Calendar** automatically takes the small yearly change in the direction of the Earth's axis into account. It is based on a period of time called the **tropical year** which is about 20 minutes less than the time it takes for the Earth to orbit the Sun exactly once. There are a fraction under 365¼ **mean solar days** in a tropical year.

So, just as there aren't exactly twelve synodic months in a year, there aren't exactly 365 days either. Different societies and religions dealt with these problems in different ways, and developed different calendars.

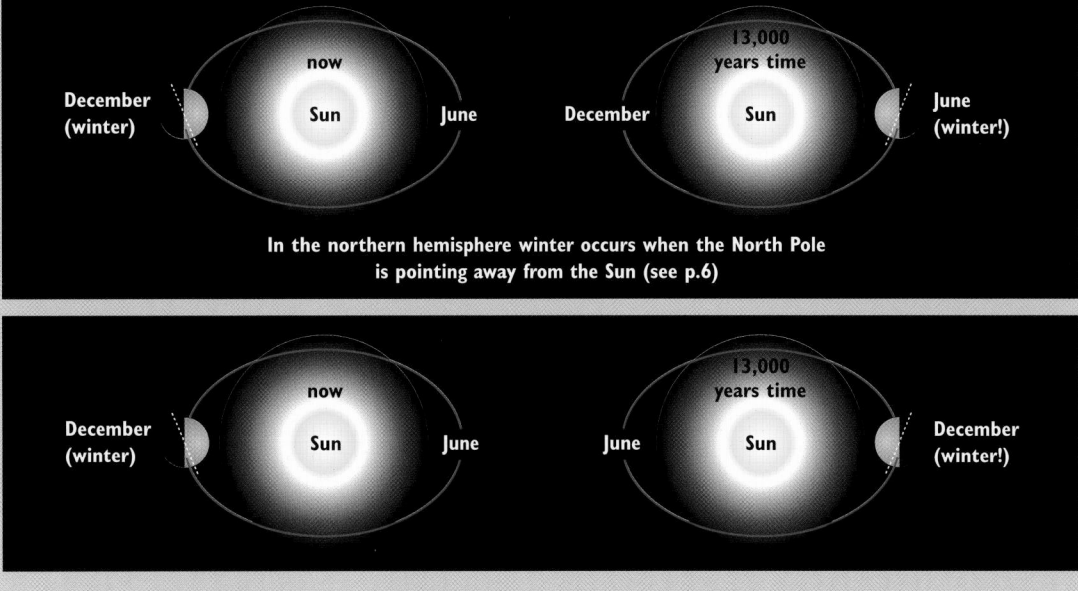

December (winter) — Sun — now — June

13,000 years time — December — Sun — June (winter!)

In the northern hemisphere winter occurs when the North Pole is pointing away from the Sun (see p.6)

December (winter) — Sun — now — June

13,000 years time — June — Sun — December (winter!)

The upper diagram shows what would happen if our year was based on the 365.256 days it takes for the Earth to go round the Sun. The length of our year (365.242 days) has been chosen so that it is always winter in the northern hemisphere in December.

The Gregorian Calendar

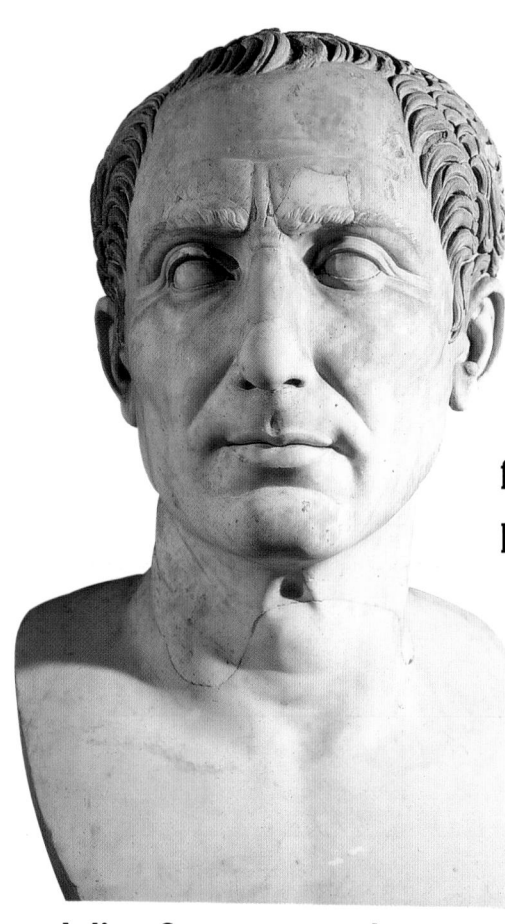

Julius Caesar started our system of leap years over 2000 years ago.

By the start of the twentieth century, although many people were still using different calendars for religious purposes, most people across the world made use of the **Gregorian Calendar** – the calendar that very nearly everyone uses today. The Gregorian Calendar developed from the Roman Calendar, and first came into use in 1582. Apart from February all the months have ended up slightly longer than a **synodic month** of 29½ days. As a result, the first day of each month does not stay in step with the appearance of a new crescent moon.

The Julian Calendar

In the year 46**BC**, the Roman dictator Julius Caesar modified the Roman Calendar. He started the system of **leap years**, with every fourth year having 366 rather than 365 days – the leap years being those whose year number is divisible by four. The calendar he devised is known as the **Julian Calendar**.

Caesar's rule about leap years didn't quite work though. For it to work perfectly, the **tropical year** would have had to be exactly 365¼ days long. At a fraction under 365¼ days it was, of course, slightly too short. The eleven minute error in the length of the year slowly started to add up, and as the years went by, the months and the seasons started to get out of step. By the year 1582, according to the calendar, the first day of spring was occurring 10 days too early (on 11 March instead of on 21 March in the northern hemisphere).

The Gregorian Calendar

Pope Gregory XIII, after whom the Gregorian Calendar is named, made two changes to the Julian Calendar. Firstly, it was advanced by 10 days so that the day following 4 October 1582 was not 5 October, but 15 October! Secondly, a slight change was made to the rule about leap years. The new rules said that instead of every fourth year being a leap year, the years whose year number ends in −00 (which are divisible by 4) would only be leap years if they were also divisible by 400, so although the year 2000 will be a leap year, the year 2100 will not.

Pope Gregory XIII changed the rules about leap years in 1582.

In this painting by William Hogarth, the injured man has his foot on a poster which says, 'Give us our 11 days'.

Although most Catholic countries were quick to make the change, non-Catholic countries weren't too keen at first. The British, who were Protestants, resisted for over 150 years. By the time the British decided to switch to the Gregorian Calendar in 1752, the calendar was eleven days out with the seasons. When 14 September immediately followed 2 September, there were cries of 'Give us back our eleven days!' and riots on the streets of London.

The Jewish and the Muslim
Calendars

The new moon

The length of each Jewish and Muslim month is closely linked to the **synodic month** of 29 days, 12 hours and 44 minutes, or just over 29½ days. The first day of each month normally coincides with the appearance of a new crescent moon in the sky. Each new day begins at sunset.

The Muslim Calendar

The Muslim year has twelve months consisting alternately of 30 and 29 days, or an average of 29½ days, making 354 days altogether. The average length of each month is about 44 minutes less than the actual length of a synodic month. These 44 minute blocks of time add up month by month, totalling just under nine hours in a year. If the calendar wasn't adjusted from time to time to allow for this, the new crescent moon would appear later and later each month as the years went by. To prevent this from happening, roughly every third year has an extra day inserted at the end of the twelfth month, making it 30 rather than 29 days long.

Each Muslim year is about eleven days shorter than the **tropical year** on which the **Gregorian Calendar** is based. Unlike the Gregorian Calendar, the Muslim Calendar does not stay in step with

The start of each Jewish and Muslim month coincides with the appearance of a thin crescent moon in the sky.

Muharram	(30 days)
Safar	(29 days)
Rabi I	(30 days)
Rabi II	(29 days)
Jumada I	(30 days)
Jumada II	(29 days)
Rajab	(30 days)
Shaban	(29 days)
Ramadan	(30 days)
Shawwal	(29 days)
Dhu al-Qadah	(30 days)
Dhu al-Hijjah	(29 or 30 days)

The twelve months of the Muslim year. The ninth month, Ramadan is the fasting month.

the seasons. The Muslim new year sometimes falls in the summer, sometimes in the spring, sometimes in the winter and sometimes in the autumn. According to the Gregorian Calendar, each Muslim year starts around eleven days earlier than the one before.

The Jewish Calendar

The Jewish Calendar is more complex. It too, has months consisting alternately of 30 and 29 days. Some years have twelve months like the Muslim Calendar, but other years have thirteen. On this basis a twelve month year would consist of 354 days – roughly eleven days less than a **tropical year** (of about 365¼ days), and a thirteen month year would consist of 384 days – roughly nineteen days more than a tropical year. To make the average length 365 days, twelve out of every nineteen years have twelve months, and seven have thirteen.

In some years, the calendar is adjusted by adding or subtracting a day. As a result, years of twelve months can have either 353, 354 or 355 days, and years of thirteen months can have 383, 384 or 385 days. Unlike the Muslim Calendar, the Jewish Calendar keeps more or less in step with the seasons.

Tishri	(30 days)
Heshvan	(29 or 30 days)
Kislev	(29 or 30 days)
Tevet	(29 days)
Shevat	(30 days)
Adar	(29 or 30 days)
Nisan	(30 days)
Iyar	(29 days)
Sivan	(30 days)
Tammuz	(29 days)
Av	(30 days)
Elul	(29 days)

The twelve months of the Jewish year. In some years, a thirteenth month Adar Sheni is added after Adar.

Centuries and Millenniums

The decision to count years from the birth of Christ, was made over 500 years after he was born. The Catholic monk Dionysius Exiguus (or literally Dennis the Short) worked out that Jesus had been born on 25 December of the Roman year 753AUC – counting from the founding of the city of Rome. He therefore renamed 1 January 754AUC as 1 January AD1. Many scholars now believe that Jesus was born a few years earlier.

Counting years

For many people, the start of a new **century** or **millennium** is a time for special celebrations. The different calendars in use count their years from different starting-points. These usually coincided with an event that was particularly important to the religion or society concerned. The Ancient Egyptians began at year one whenever a new pharaoh was crowned, so no one ever celebrated the start of a new century let alone a new millennium.

Counting forwards and backwards

The starting-point for the **Gregorian Calendar** is Jesus Christ's birth. **BC** stands for *before Christ,* and is used when years are counted backwards from Christ's birth, for example 46BC. Some people prefer to use BCE instead. It stands for *before the common era.* **AD** stands for *anno Domini,* which means 'in the year of our Lord'. It is used when we want to make it clear that the year referred to has been counted from Christ's birth. Some people prefer to use CE which stands for *common era* instead. The date 16 July AD622 coincides with the start of year one of the Muslim Calendar, which began when the prophet Muhammad escaped from his enemies in Mecca.

A new millennium

The first century AD began at the start of year one, the second century AD began at the start of the year 101, and in the same way, the twentieth century began at the start of the year 1901. The start of the Universal Day on 1 January, 1901 (when it was midnight on the **Prime Meridian** at Greenwich), marked the exact moment that the twentieth century 'officially' began.

Although the twenty-first century, and third millennium, will begin at the start of 1 January 2001, most of the world will celebrate a year early at the start of the year 2000. Greenwich will be at the centre of these celebrations. The year AD2000 begins in the fourth month of the Jewish year 5760, and the ninth month of the Muslim year 1420.

1 January 1998. The Eiffel Tower in Paris shows that it is the 730th day before the start of the year 2000.

The countdown clock on the Prime Meridian at the Greenwich **observatory** showing 932 days to go until the start of the year 2000.

At the end of 1999, many computers will reset their calendar to the year 1900 or 1980. This problem is known as the millennium bug. It will occur as a result of the way in which the computers have been programmed. Many people are concerned about the effect it might have on computers used in transport systems, hospital equipment and businesses.

Glossary

AD (Anno Domini) normally used with a year number to indicate how long after Christ's birth an event occurred, also called CE (Common Era)

am (ante meridiem) a time which occurs in the morning before 12.00

atomic clock the most accurate type of clock available. The best will lose or gain no more than one second in 10,000,000 years.

atomic time time which comes to us via an atomic clock

AUC (Ab Urbe Condita) used by the Romans, with a year number, to indicate how long after the founding of the city of Rome an event occurred

axis the imaginary line running through the centre of the Earth between the North and the South Poles, around which the Earth spins. It can also mean any line around which an object spins.

balance wheel an oscillating wheel, used with a balance spring in some clocks and watches to make them tick at the right rate

BC (Before Christ) normally used with a year number to indicate how long before Christ's birth an event occurred, also called BCE (Before the Common Era)

caesium a soft, silvery metal whose atomic properties enable extremely accurate timekeepers (atomic clocks) to be made

century a period of 100 years

chart name for a map used by sailors

chronometer a portable clock, which is able to keep accurate time, usually at sea, and which is normally set to Greenwich Mean Time wherever on the Earth's surface it is being used

Co-ordinated Universal Time (UTC) the time on which most clocks around the world are now based. It never varies by more than 0.9 seconds from Greenwich Mean Time or Universal Time.

Equator the imaginary line around the centre of the Earth that separates the northern from the southern hemisphere

escapement a device which makes a clock mechanism turn with a series of stop-start movements or ticks

foliot a swinging bar, used by the first clockmakers to make their clocks tick at the right rate

Greenwich Mean Time (GMT) the local mean time at Greenwich, and the standard time originally used by the whole of the UK

Gregorian Calendar the name given to the Julian Calendar after it had been modified by Pope Gregory XIII in 1582. It is the calendar currently in use by most people around the world.

International Date Line an imaginary line that runs through the Pacific Ocean. Passengers crossing towards the west put their watches forwards by a day, whilst those going towards the east put them back by a day.

Julian Calendar the name given to the Roman Calendar after it had been modified by Julius Caesar in 46BC

latitude a measure of how far north or south of the Equator something is

leap second a second that is occasionally added to clocks to ensure that they stay in step with the spinning (but generally slowing) Earth

leap year a year of 366 rather than the more usual 365 days (as counted by the Gregorian or Julian Calendar). They usually happen every 4 years.

local apparent time the time shown by a sundial

local time time linked to the position of the Sun in the sky. At any given moment, the further east you are, the later the local time.

longitude a measure of how far east or west of the Prime Meridian at Greenwich something is

mean solar day the average length of a solar day, and equal in time to 24 hours

mean time time measurement based on the mean solar day of 24 hours

meridian (line) any north-south line, either imaginary or real, on the Earth's surface

midday the time when the Sun reaches its highest point of the day (and crosses from the east side of the meridian to the west). A sundial will show 12.00 when this happens.

millennium a period of 1000 years

Nautical Almanac a book of tables which allowed sailors to calculate the time at Greenwich from observations of the Moon's position against the background of stars

observatory a building from which astronomers make observations of the stars with telescopes and other instruments

orbit the path of a planet around the Sun or the Moon around the Earth

oscillation a side to side movement of a vibrating or swinging object, for example a pendulum

pendulum a swinging wooden or metal rod with a bob (weight) attached to its lower end, used in some clocks to make them tick at the correct rate

phases of the Moon the name given to the changing appearance of the Moon as it orbits the Earth. The phases include: new moon, first quarter, full moon and last quarter.

pm (post meridiem) a time which occurs in the afternoon or evening (after 12.00)

precession the gradual change in direction of the axis of rotation of a spinning object such as the Earth or a top

Prime Meridian the north-south line running from the North to the South Pole through the observatory at Greenwich, and the line from which east and west are now measured

quartz a crystalline mineral found in many types of rock. Quartz can be made to oscillate and is used in some clocks to make them 'tick' at the right rate.

sidereal day the time it takes for the Earth to spin round once (through 360°) on its axis. Equal in time to about 4 minutes less than a mean solar or 'normal' day

sidereal year the time it takes for the Earth to go around the Sun once – equal in time to 365.256 days

solar day the period of time between one midday (or midnight) and the next. The Earth turns through about 361° on its axis from one solar day to the next. Solar or natural days, vary slightly in length throughout the year because of the way in which the Earth orbits the Sun.

standard time an agreed time to which all clocks in a country or part of a country are set (rather than setting them all to local time)

summer time the standard time used in some countries during the summer months in order to make better use of the hours of daylight. It is normally one hour ahead of the standard time used for the rest of the year.

sundial a device that makes use of shadows to find the time from the Sun's position in the sky

synodic month the period of time between one new moon and the next – equal in time to just over 29½ days

temperate zones the two regions of the Earth between the tropics and the polar zones

time zone the Earth is divided into 24 time zones. In each zone, clocks are set to the same standard time – normally a whole number of hours ahead of or behind Co-ordinated Universal Time.

transit telescope a telescope mounted along its own meridian, so that it can swing up and down (pointing northwards or southwards), but not from side to side. They were used in the past to find the time and to measure star positions.

tropical year the year length on which the Gregorian Calendar is based – equal in time to 365.242 days, and shorter than a sidereal year as it takes into account the precession of the Earth's axis

tropics the region of the Earth close to the equator (bounded by the lines of latitude 23.5° North and 23.5° South)

Universal Time (UT) another name for Greenwich Mean Time. The Universal Day starts at midnight on the Greenwich meridian.

Index